A Hobo

And

The poor rich man.

Thulani Ngwenya

A Hobo and The Poor Rich Man

Copyright © 2020 Thulani Ngwenya

First edition 2020
ISBN 9781983077425

All rights reserved
No part of this work may be reproduced or transmitted in any form or by any means, electronic, photographic or mechanical, including photocopying and recording on record, tape or laser disk, on microfilm, via the Internet, by e-mail, or by any other information storage or retrieval system, without prior written permission from the copyright owner.

The author has made every effort to obtain permission for and acknowledge the use of copyrighted material. Refer all enquiries to the author.

The views reflected are not necessarily those of the printer.

Acknowledgements

I would like to thank God the creator, the Consciousness, the Spirit, the Being, the Higher Power, the natural power that runs the world, the awareness, the I AM, the one who caused me to be here for the experiences I've encountered in my journey of life.

It is through these experiences that this book could be written because I have solid experiences to refer to. I also want to thank God for the inspiration and guidance from the start to the end of this book. Sometimes there was no inspiration and I would wait for days, but when God did inspire, the pages were filled. At times there was no inspiration at all, I would wait on God for days until he inspired my writing, and so, the pages were filled.

I also thank you, the reader, for acquiring this book and I hope its contents will shake your faith as they did to mine when I was writing it.

Special thanks

A special thank you to **Khanyisile Sibiya** for the magnificent editing.

Anything else is my own fault.

Introduction

Once or twice or maybe three times in your "lifetime" you come across a book that challenges your way of thinking and changes "your" life remarkably in a way you've always desired but never thought was "possible". The reason some texts are put in quotes is simply because as we dive deeper you will learn that their meaning changes as you read further

This may be one of those books. The intention of this book is to reveal unto and help you remember who you truly are. To reveal unto you your relationship with the ALL, that some choose to call God and bring to your attention that you are complete and have it all. You are limitless. When it comes to what you can do, what you can achieve and more importantly, what you can be; there are no limits.

Many books have been written on this subject. I personally have read many such books and what I've learned is that though they may all be addressing the same topic; they all are individually very important in your journey to remembrance. As Buddha once said, "When the student is ready, the teacher will appear." It is therefore not an accident that you are reading this book right now.

It was meant to happen. You are the student; you are ready for its content. And the book is your teacher for this part of your journey.

Generally human beings spend the greater part of their existence avoiding the things, they desire for the fear of death, only to learn later in life when they are closer to death that there is no death. This is the wisdom attributed to age. It is said that the older you get, the wiser you become. Blessed are those who find this truth or are found by it in the days of their youth for the rest of their existence is changed to living. It is important to note the difference between the two, to *exist* and to *live*. The choice of whether to live or to exist stems from the understanding of who you are. For everything you do is influenced by you. That is to say by who you know you are.

Perhaps halfway through the book you would have realized that who you are is no different from everyone else. The reason we seem different is because people generally identify themselves with their thoughts. Note from this statement that because it is said "your thoughts", that implies the thoughts must belong to someone, we can say the owner of the thoughts. This therefore means that you are not your thoughts. This same question is birthed by statements people use when referring to parts of "their" bodies; *my eyes, my arms, my ears, my birth, my soul,* etc. One can use the "my" referring to all parts, so when you ask, who is the "my"? One usually does not get a clear answer.

It is therefore partly the reason this book was written, to help you answer who the "my' is, and more importantly to reveal to you that you are limitless. Generally, people refer to the collective, that is, all parts of their body joined together as the answer to who the "my" is. But then that is also nullified when they refer to the whole body as "my" body. All suffering and all limitations stem from the identification of self with the "my" referring to the physical body. But if that is not who you are, then who are you?

A hobo and the poor rich man

#

*"Sometimes we see a Hobo with dead black eyes
We think to ourselves, how sad he must be*

*This truth is he's burned out from all the excitement and joy
You see he has seen all there is to see, not known by you and me*

*He's just recharging to go on another Adventure
He's not one to pity, it is us that he pities, as he looks up and says,
more coffee please."*

Unknown.

Ray

"Your talent is God's gift to you. What you do with it is your gift back to God."

It was a chilly winter afternoon in the streets of Jo'burg. I was just about to wrap up my day when a homeless man walked straight to me with his head facing down. In that part of the world, homeless people are referred to as Hobos and are known for many mischievous habits including criminal activities. My first instincts were telling me to cross over to the other side of the road to avoid the hobo, but then, I also thought that this could be my opportunity to do something good, spare some change or buy the man something to eat.

To my surprise the man greeted me with respect and I couldn't but stop to listen to what he had to say. The man was dirty and smelly as could be expected. He had long hair and a very long beard with his skin looking a bit cracked and shrunken with wrinkles. He looked like he could be in his fifties, if my judgment was anything to go by. Dressed in multiple layers of clothing, he looked comfortably warm in this cold winter afternoon.

"My name is Raymond, Raymond Jackson. My friends call me Ray."

He said as he stretched his hand towards me for a handshake waiting for me to respond with a similar gesture. Looking at the hand, I had doubts, so I opted for a fist bump instead.

"Nice to meet you Ray." I replied. "Keith Coleman."

With a very soft humble voice Ray replied; "It is a pleasure to meet you Mr. Coleman. My sincere apologies for bothering you this afternoon."

And I was deeply touched, looking at this hobo so humble towards me, a young man young enough to be his son. I felt compelled to oblige and give this man my full attention.

"Please call me Keith." I said with a smile. "How can I help you this afternoon Ray?"

"A conversation." Ray replied.

I didn't understand what he meant so I asked; "What do you mean Ray, I don't understand."

"If you could allow me a few minutes to speak with you sir, a few minutes are all I ask." He said.

Thinking about the short encounter and my already formed perception of the man, I thought I could spare a few minutes for a conversation. After all, it isn't much. And it definitely is something I can afford. So, I agreed and invited Ray to a park near-by.

I must admit this was totally unexpected. Experience had taught me that hobos generally want money or food. They never ask for anything else. In my head I was wondering what this man wanted to speak to me about. I did think it had everything to do with how I could help him get off the streets and change his life. I was already thinking about possible ways by which I could assist this man who seemed very kind too. I was trying to figure out in my head what tragedy could have befallen Ray for him to find himself on the cold streets of Jo'burg.

We had just sat down when as if Ray was reading my thoughts, breaking the silence he said; "It was my doing Keith, it was the choices I made that landed me on the cold streets of Jo'burg."

Curios to learn what could have happened I asked; "What do you mean you chose this life Ray?"

I couldn't imagine anybody choosing a hard life on the streets instead of a warm comfortable home. Hobos are known to live off trash. They eat from trash; wear trash and use trash for shelter. How could a sane human being see trash as the best way to spend their days on earth?

"You know Keith; I've been watching you for some time now. You remind me a lot of myself when I was your age. Bold, ambitious, courageous and sorry to say but I also had a big ego too, just like you." Ray started.

"Regardless to say I admire what you've done with your business, Colemans. I love that coffee shop."

It was a huge surprise to me hearing a homeless man comparing me to himself. I am a businessman. Though I do not operate a multibillion-dollar corporation, I still run a very successful coffee shop. How dare he compares himself to me?

"Forgive me Keith, I do not mean at all to disrespect you. I admire you and am afraid you are going down the path I travelled. So, if you will, I'd love to share with you the lessons I learned throughout my journey. Sometimes you don't have to make the same mistakes if you can learn from others' you know."

I nodded my head quietly with no response.

Ray continued. "And I strongly believe you are still too far from reaching your potential. There is a lot more you can still achieve personally and in your business. You are a brilliant young man Keith. And I know this is not at all what you would have expected to hear from a hobo."

Ray was right. I could have never imagined myself receiving advice, let alone being coached by a hobo. After all, if he is so brilliant, could he not do something to get out of the streets? My emotions were mixed, I didn't know whether to sit here and listen to this man or if I should stand up and go.

Somehow Ray realized my discomfort and trying to have me settled he continued. "You know Keith; our ego is one of the biggest reasons we all fail in life. Your ego is probably already telling you not to listen to a hobo, but your instincts contradict. Follow your instincts. That's my advice." Ray paused.

"I would really love to help you Keith, if you may allow me."

I was curious to hear what Ray had to say, but this man had hi-jacked me. I hadn't planned for this and already it was getting pretty late.

"I know that this was totally unplanned but if you will, meet me here tomorrow morning before you head to your store. I will be here tomorrow waiting. Go home and think about it. Don't let your ego get in the way. If you will allow me, I will see you here tomorrow morning. It was an absolute pleasure meeting you Keith. I look forward to getting to know you better."

Ray stood up and slowly walked away without echoing another word. I remained sitting for a good twenty minutes after he'd left trying to make sense of what had just happened.

The whole night I couldn't stop thinking about Ray. Something deep within told me that spending time with Ray was of utmost importance. I was convinced it was good for me. Ray would be my teacher for the next few weeks, a homeless man with wisdom to impart on me. I must say I was excited and curious at the same time. The night seemed so long. I was looking forward to spending time with Ray for some strange reason.

A hobo and the poor rich man

A hobo and the poor rich man

A hobo and the poor rich man

"Drowning in my inner self,
I've awaken to a new world,
the one I always wanted, the one I never got.

Here lies my happiness,
my reason to smile,
I pursued my bliss, long after it died.

I've left my fears behind,
far behind to trail me back,
I stand here with confidence, that I thought I lacked.

I've shattered the perm of failure,
I look forward to success,
with self-ignited light, that I dearly caress.

I've explored myself right here,
found the true me,
have learnt the meaning of life and the reason to cherish it.

Drowning in my inner self,
I've awaken to my world,
the one where I met myself, the one I'd never leave again."

Ruchita Sharma

A meeting with myself
"God is the originator of life."

The next morning, I woke up earlier than I usually do. I suppose it was the curiosity and excitement to spend time with a hobo as a mentor for my life and business. I couldn't stop wondering though why Ray had chosen me. But someone once said, "everything happens for a reason." Though I didn't know what the reason was, I trusted and believed that this was very necessary at this stage in my life.

Thinking about this, I realized that I actually didn't have anyone I call a coach or a mentor, so maybe Ray was sent to occupy this gap.

On my way to work just as Ray had suggested, I went straight to the park first to meet with him. Getting closer I realized that Ray was concentrating, not looking at me approach. When I got close enough, I saw that his eyes were closed, and he was humming melodies. I chose not to disturb and waited for him to finish.

"Good morning Keith, a beautiful morning indeed isn't it." Ray greeted. "I'm glad you came my friend; I am looking forward to spending some time with you. I just finished my daily morning ritual and ready to get started, please have a seat." Ray said as he pointed to a mat that was laid on the grass.

Though Ray still looked like a hobo, he seemed to have cleaned up today and his face glowing with so much energy that I felt when I stared at him.

"Morning Ray. It is a very cold morning, but beautiful I suppose. What do you mean you've just completed your daily morning ritual?" I replied not understanding what Ray meant by this. I hoped this was not some kind of a cult with rituals I'd have to follow in order to reach my potential.

Sensing my concern Ray replied. "Relax my friend, there's nothing to worry about. Every morning I connect with the creator of all things before I start my day. That's what I mean. It is important to align yourself with the natural powers that run the world you know Keith, in order to make sure that your efforts are guided and achieve the intended results. Do you believe there is a creator Keith?"

With hesitation in my voice I replied, "Yes I do Ray, I believe someone created all this." I said pointing around referring to the nature surrounding us.

"That's brilliant." Piped Ray. "Someone created all this, someone created you too you know. You know Keith in order for you to reach your full potential; you must first be exposed to your potential. You must know what you have first before you can use it. Otherwise it will all be there available for you to use, but because you do not know you have it, it will be as good as not there at all. For it is written; '*My people perish because of lack of knowledge.*'"

"What do you mean Ray? I think I know everything I have; I mean, I'm the one who makes the decisions to acquire all the tools I need. So, I'm sure I utilize all that I know I have."

Ray looked at me and smiled.

"You have to know where you come from, you must know the building blocks holding you together. You must know who you are, and that does not mean who your parents are and what your last name is. This is the wisdom I'd like to share with you today. Because until you know who you truly are, you will never know what you have and thus never be able to reach your full potential."

I must admit that this sounded a bit strange to me, but I believed there was a lot of wisdom I was about to receive. I sat attentively looking at Ray and listening to what he was saying with much curiosity.

"Here, take this." Ray offered as he handed me a journal and a pen. "It is very important to keep a journal Keith. I need you to make notes of everything that comes to mind during our encounter. Make notes of everything you will learn from me."

"Thank you, Ray." I said as I received the journal. I must say I was already submitting to the instructions of my strange homeless master. I was willing to let go and allow myself to be taught.

"It is written; '*In the beginning was the Word, and the Word was with God, and the Word was God. All things were made by him; and without him was not anything made that was made.*'"

Ray proceeded. "The intention of this quote Keith is for you to comprehend the power of the one who created all things. It is said nothing was created without Him. Can you even begin to imagine the possibilities if you possessed the same power as the creator? Can you begin to imagine the things you would do and what you could be?"

My mind started wondering; overwhelmed by what could be if I possessed such power. I was already imagining the possibilities. It was like there was a fire started within me. I felt like a superhuman.

"My life would be so amazing; I can't even start imagining." I replied with my eyes focused on one direction as if I was looking attentively at something.

"The creator used words to create all that was created. He commanded the light to come into existence; *'Let there be light.'* He said. And there was light."

"Amazing."

That was the only thing I could say, with my eyes still focused.

"You know Keith; you have that power. You have the power to create, by your words you can and already have been commanding things into existence."

"I do?" I queried, not fully grasping what Ray was saying.

"Yes, you do. You have been doing it for years. Look at your business for instance, first it was a thought and then you either said it to yourself or told someone about it by a spoken word and, and so it became. Your thoughts are also words spoken silently."

"But I thought that it was my hard work that helped me build my business?" I interjected.

"Your hard work was just a part of the process; it was a tool to fulfill your spoken word. You are that powerful. You are created with the same material, the same building blocks as the creator if I may say so."

"Please elaborate Ray." I asked changing my sitting to make sure I fully get what Ray is saying.

"To clarify this Keith, allow me to make a few quotes from scribes."

"Sure." I replied.

"The scribes have written: in the fourteenth book of Deuteronomy; '*You are the children of the Lord your God.*' And in the third book of the first epistle of John it is written; '...*dear friends, now are we the children of God.*' and lastly in the seventeenth book of the Acts; '*...For we are also his offspring.*'"

I nodded my head in agreement allowing Ray to continue.

"All these confirm one thing Keith, we are the children of the creator. We are his or her offspring. But still do not fully tell us who we are or how we are unless we know how the creator is."

"I was just about to ask." I said still not understanding what all this meant.

"You see Keith, God is spirit. If we were created in his image and likeness and are her offspring, what do you think that makes us?" Asked Ray.

"Spirit, that makes us spirit. Speaking from my knowledge of what an offspring is, an offspring of spirit is spirit and nothing else." I replied, somehow getting where Ray was heading.

"Hundred percent Keith." Ray responded, somehow impressed with my answer.

"That is correct, we are spirit. But we spend our lives unconscious, living in the body if I may say. We live without awareness, identifying ourselves with the flesh we can touch. But the truth is, that is not who we are. We are the life that entered the body, and not the body itself. In other words, we are the consciousness."

"I get that." I responded.

This was deep for me. I never looked at it that way. But now that Ray has explained it, it makes a lot of sense.

I continued, "What I still do not understand though is; what does all this have to do with me reaching my full potential?"

I was still trying to put things together and needed Ray to elaborate, to help me understand.

"Great question." Echoed Ray.

"The secret is that you already have everything you need. What must still happen is for you to realize this. It is for you to be aware of all that you have, all that you are."

Giving Ray a look of surprise he continued, "If God is everywhere, if he is in all, and if you are just like him and are her offspring, shouldn't you have access to all that he has access to?"

"There is nowhere God can be that you cannot be, that is your nature. Because we are consciousness, we are not the physical. We are the collective that is God. We bring things into existence. Hence it is written to do unto another as you wish done unto self. For what you do to another, you do unto self. You and I cannot be separated. We are one. We are God."

"If you go back to the seventeenth chapter of the book of Acts, the scribes have written that *'in him we live, in him we move and in him we have our being'*. Jesus the Christ confirmed this as well when he said we are one with him for he and the father are one."

"Do you mean to tell me that I created all this?" I asked.

"Not you, God created all this. Consciousness; the natural power that runs the world. You are consciousness Keith; not just you, we are consciousness. We, God created all this. Before Abraham was, we were."

I paused for a second trying to digest this and take it all in. "But how?" Finally, I asked. "

I understand that this is all new for you Keith, but with time it will all make sense." Responded Ray.

"What you need to take from all this though is that whatever God has access to, you too have access to. Can you tell me anything that you think God does not have access to? Is there anything you think God cannot do?"

As if he was not waiting for an answer Ray continued, "There is nothing God cannot do, be or have. It all belongs to Him. It all belongs to you. Because you are spirit, you are consciousness; you are God's offspring. Where he is, you are. What he is, you are. And what he has, you have."

"This is a lot to take in Ray. This is all new to me. I never saw things this way. This is deep." I said; sharing how I felt with this new perspective I've just learned about.

Already my view had been shifted; I had already started seeing things differently.

"This is enough for today. I have revealed to you what you already knew but had forgotten. I've shared with you who you are and what you are made of. It has been brought forth for you the power you possess, the power you are, for by who you are, your nature tells you, you have everything you need."

"I think this is enough for our first session Keith. I appreciate that you have been taking notes. I urge you that during your spare time today, and this afternoon when you get home. Go over what we've discussed here today. Note any uncertainties or questions you may have, and I'll be happy to clarify those for you tomorrow."

"I will see you at the same time tomorrow. Go and be great, your customers need that awesomeness." Ray said with a huge green.

"Thank you so much Ray, this has totally shifted my perspective. I will certainly do as you say. What are you going to do today?" I asked as I stood up preparing to leave.

"The life of a hobo is not so complicated you know." Ray said with a big smile.

We exchanged our good-byes and I went my way. I left Ray still sitting at the park possibly planning his day further or doing what he always does.

A hobo and the poor rich man

A hobo and the poor rich man

#

*"One God, many faces.
One family, many races.
One truth, many paths.
One heart, many complexions.
One light, many reflections.
One world, many imperfections.
ONE.
We are all one,
But many."*

Suzy Kassem

One with the All
"I am in the father and the father is in me."

The whole day after I'd seen Ray I couldn't stop thinking about what I had learned. Sometimes during work I'd be absent minded that it would be easily apparent to my colleagues. The more I thought about it though, the more it made sense. It is a lot similar to what I have heard about the teaching of the Buddha. The Buddha taught that we are one. He taught that we must get rid of the idea of "I" and "mine".

When I think about it, it doesn't seem to be possible to prove the oneness in the physical. The oneness does seem possible though if indeed we are consciousness, if we are spirit. Because if we are spirit, where can one separate multiple pieces of the spirit to create a lot of "us"?

The following morning, I was up at five o'clock. I was excited to meet Ray, curious to learn what this great homeless teacher of mine had prepared for me today. Though I still wondered to myself why Ray had chosen me, and how long he had been observing me for, as he said that he'd been watching me for a while. I chose not to question him and submit to this lesson; I strongly felt that what Ray was teaching was relevant and required at this point in my life.

Arriving at the park I found Ray finishing his meditation. "Good to see you Keith, welcome. Please take a seat."

"Good morning Ray, are you well this morning?" I asked.

"Always awesome Keith, always awesome; especially after my morning exercise. I feel fresh and so energized."

"You exercise?" I asked with so much amaze.

"Your body is a temple of God Keith, of course I exercise this body. Otherwise dwelling in it would be undesirable. Bodily exercise is good for you."

What else does this homeless man do? I wondered. Ray does all the things one wouldn't expect from a homeless man. Curious to know more about Ray's homelessness I asked.

"So where do you actually stay Ray?

"Foxes have holes and the birds of the air have nests, but the son of man hath nowhere to lay his head." That was Ray's reply.

"I'll let you in on that later Keith. I hope you've had some time to reflect on the lessons of yesterday."

"If you'd allow me, I'd like to move on with what has been prepared for you today, unless you have needs to clarify what you've already learned?"

"Actually, it all made sense when I took some time to reflect Ray. I couldn't believe I've known this all along. Please continue."

"A story has been told of a young man who had lived with his father, in his presence since birth." Ray started.

"During the time he was in his father's presence, he lacked nothing. All his needs were taken care of. Never once did he feel he had needs that were not met. So, when he grew old, thinking he was wiser, he went to his father and asked; 'father, please give me my portion of your inheritance so that I can leave and be on my own.'"

"Though saddened in his heart the father respected the wishes of his son. And so, he did as the son had asked. He gave him a portion and embraced him with a kiss. The son bid him good-bye and he left."

"Away from the father the son wasted what his father had given him and soon it was all finished. With nothing to help him carry on, he remembered the days when he was in the presence of his father when all his needs were met. With regret in his heart, the son decided that he would go back home to his father, beg for forgiveness and ask the father to receive him back not as his son, but as one of his servants, so long he had something to eat and shelter."

"On his way he went. Closer to home the father saw him. With joy he ran to his son, embraced him and welcomed him back. He instructed his servants to prepare a feast to celebrate the return of his son."

"Seeing what was happening, with grief in his heart the older son enquired of his father; 'father, lo have I been with you all these years laboring for you. I have never disrespected you and have never asked of you to let me go from thy presence. But father never once did you give me anything to celebrate with my friends.

But this your son took everything you gave to him and wasted it, and now that he is back you prepare a big feast for him.'"

"The father, looking at him with eyes glowing with love said to him; 'son, all that I have is yours, it all belongs to you. And it has been all this time.'"

"This is what we discussed yesterday Keith. You have everything because you are one with the all, you are one with God, and all that belongs to God belongs to you too."

"What the prodigal son demonstrates in this tale is; after people have learned the truth, the truth about who they are, exactly what you have learned Keith; they live by the truth. For you shall know the truth and the truth will make you free, remaining one with the universe and conscious of the oneness. During this period, peace love and joy rule their lives. All their needs are taken care of, for they are in the presence of the Father, they are consciously aware of their relationship with God, that they are in God and he in them. During this period, they are aligned completely with the natural power that runs the world and all as God said after creating the earth, is good."

"This state of consciousness though due to many reasons usually lasts for a shorter period and that's the state where they feel they're better off without the father. People depart from the state of consciousness and for a little while all is well. But within a short space of time, suffering returns and they start to long for the days when they lived consciously. They long for the days when they were in the presence of the father, when love, peace and joy ruled. And just like the prodigal son in this tale, they are joyfully welcomed back to the state of consciousness when they seek it. And love, peace and joy rule in their lives once again."

"But why would you want to leave a place where all is well?" I asked trying to make sense of all this.

"Just as is done by great athletes Keith, practice or in this case, constant exercise of your consciousness is required for you to remain in that state. In this world the flesh, the physical body has its own desires, which are normally contradictory to yours. You need to practice the state of consciousness, living by the will of the spirit and not of the flesh, until the flesh fully submits to your will. And even at that stage, you shouldn't stop practicing. This is exactly why mediation is part of my daily ritual."

"Mediation is a way to help remain in the state of consciousness. In this state you know you have all you need. Something the older son didn't know. He had everything because he was one with the father. The prodigal son had everything when he was with the father also but lost everything when he left the presence of the father."

"Meditation and prayer are some of the methods you should use to remain one with the father, one with the universe, one with the all, one with God. Try to remain in that state."

"Jesus knew this when he said to his disciples; *'pray without ceasing, for the spirit indeed is willing but the flesh is weak'.*"

"I must say though Ray that it seems to me that the more one enters the state of consciousness, the less one needs on this earth, is that how it really is? Shouldn't the state of consciousness enable you to reach your potential to achieve your goals here on earth? I'm a bit confused there."

"If tap water came out boiling Keith, would you still need your boilers?

"No, not at all."

"That's exactly what this is about. All suffering arises from identifying yourself with the flesh, with the physical body. You worry about food to feed the body; you worry about shelter to house the body; you worry about clothes to cover the body. But now you know that you are not the body but the spirit, must you still worry about clothes to dress the spirit?" Ray asked.

"Of course not, how can one dress spirit."

"That is the point, the basics become enough to you for the body, the more you identify yourself with consciousness. Instead of desiring expensive apparel, basic descent apparel becomes enough. Instead of desiring a very expensive house, basic accommodation becomes enough for you. All because your priorities change, remaining in the state of consciousness becomes your primary desire and focus."

"But what about reaching my full potential then? You said there is still a lot I can achieve."

Though what Ray was saying made a lot of sense to me I still wanted to achieve a lot of things in my career.

"When you've entered fully the state of consciousness, you would have reached your potential Keith."

"At that stage, it is no longer a matter of faith, but a state of knowing. You no longer believe you have everything and can do anything, but you know it. At this stage nothing is impossible for you. For you are fully aware of your oneness with God, the creator of it all. And all that is impossible with men is possible with you, for it is possible with God."

"Thus, will you say unto mountains, be thou removed, and be thou cast into the sea. And the mountains will obey."

"Jesus came to teach consciousness, you would know that he had as little as possible for the body, but could do anything. He fed the hungry, healed the sick, calmed storms and a lot more."

"With him, it was not a matter of believing he could do all these, he knew he could. So, if Jesus had a career that he wanted to thrive in, do you think he would not have been able to do it?"

"Of course, he could do anything." I replied, getting what Ray was saying much clearer.

"So, if Jesus told you that he and the father are one, and that you and he are one, would you believe him?" Ray asked looking straight into my eyes.

"Yes."

"Well he said it. He said the things that he did and more you will also do, if you believe in his teachings, if you enter and remain in the state of consciousness. If you remain in spirit, one with the father."

"I get it now Ray, much clearer."

"I know you do Keith. And I'm glad you do."

"It's like when you lived in your father's house." Ray continued. "During meal-times at the dinner table when you'd ask your father to pass you the salt. Though you knew the salt belonged to your father, you didn't have to wonder whether your father would pass you the salt, you knew in your heart that he would, and he did."

"When you are one with the universe, all that you set yourself to achieve, the universe conspires to make it happen for you. It works for you. *'For I know the thoughts I think towards you, saith the Lord…'*

"So, what you're saying Ray is that all that is required of me is to live consciously and I can achieve anything."

"What I'm saying is seek ye first the kingdom, the eternal state of consciousness and everything else shall be given unto you."

"I get it Ray, this is brilliant. I love this. I love you Ray." I said in a state of excitement. This was really exciting for me, the idea that I could attain eternal peace, joy and love.

"I love you too Keith."

"So, when would you say is the right time for one to enter the state of consciousness Ray?"

"Now is the time Keith, enter now."

A hobo and the poor rich man

A hobo and the poor rich man

#

"I am not alone you see?
for everything I see is me
the trees, the mountains
and the moss covered trees
without them I would not exist
nothing in this world persists
without you either... just be still
can't you feel your cells are eager?
knowing just how much you grew
doing all those things you do
at all the perfect moments too
your energy leaves deep imprints
within the grooves of all existence
the fallen leaves can feel your truth
the sky forms colours pink to blues
just as your heart loves to do
the sun seeks darkness to shine through
all you bloom
the world is spinning
all for you."

Oellobeautiful

Living consciously
"For to be carnally minded is death; but to be spiritually minded is life and peace."

I spent most of my evening thinking about my last meeting with Ray. I had the opportunity to reflect on what he said about my full potential. When I thought about it, there were many things I have done in life without doubting in my mind that I could do them. And when I look deeply, it is in those little moments that I am in tune with the universe. In those little moments I fully let go and trust.

An example of this is when I walk. Taking one foot forward after the other I do not worry whether they'll lend properly on the ground and propel me in my direction. I just walk, and my feet carry me safely on my path.

I like the example Ray used about the dinner table. It is very true. I knew when I was young that everything that belonged to my father belonged to me too. I never doubted for a second that if I ask of my father for certain things he would refuse. Sometimes I never even had to ask, I just took what I needed when I needed, and my father would be ok with it. In fact, he never even reminded me that they were his possessions and not mine, in my eyes, all that was his was mine too.

The following morning, I tried meditating for a little while. Though I had not fully understood the method, I just sat quietly allowing the mind to be still. It felt great. I also made a promise to myself that I would start exercising every morning.

Arriving at the park that morning I found Ray preparing a game of Monopoly. I knew very well that this was meant for a great lesson today. I already trusted Ray as a teacher full of wisdom, so I didn't question his methods.

Kindly I greeted Ray and sat down on the mat prepared for me.

"Are we playing a game this morning Ray?" I asked to break the ice.

"Of course, we are Keith, not this one you see here though." Ray said as he continued laying the cards on the board.

"Playing is as important as anything else Keith. Play and play often. Do not keep the kid in you hidden. Let him out."

"You know Keith; peace is what we are all after. We all desire peace, love and joy eternal."

"People generally rely on the works of their hands, the works of the flesh to acquire such peace. We want jobs with the hope that when we finally earn wages we will afford a comfortable life, which means we will acquire our desired peace."

"A comfortable life for instance may be viewed as a new home or a new car. Often when one eventually does get a job and can afford a new home, suddenly there are other newer responsibilities that come with the new home. When they visualised their lives in the new home, they did not anticipate all the extra responsibilities that come with it."

"In the new home there are bills to be paid to keep the home running. Suddenly, there are security concerns to protect the property in the home and to protect the home itself. This cycle continues for the rest of our lives on earth. We are never satisfied. The more we acquire, the more we want.

The job that we so desired might also come with its own challenges, instead of one acquiring the desired peace, people end up stressing often because of the challenges in the new job."

"We let our lives be just like this game of Monopoly. The winner in this game is the one who acquires the most until all his opponents are completely bankrupt. But during the acquisition, you worry about the possibilities of losing what you have already acquired. So the focus is not on being happy with what you've acquired so far. But about worrying a lot more until you've acquired everything."

"Imagine if you owned everything Keith, would you be happy to see everyone else suffer because you have taken it all?"

"I would be very sad Ray." I said, imagining what that picture would look like.

"We can continue counting some of the things that people desire with the hope that they'll get peace; relationships, more money, material possessions, power, status, etc. But as have been indicated, it is very rare if at all, that any of these things ever bring the desired peace. The reason for this is that peace, like joy, and love are spiritual fruits. They spring out of the spirit, out of consciousness."

"This does not necessarily mean that people must not have goals to work towards. It simply means that with the understanding and knowledge of who we are, we must never be attached to anything or anyone on this earth. Our happiness must not depend on our material possessions or earthly relationships. We must be prepared to lose it all and still be happy."

"This reminds me of the story of a certain rich man who desired to enter into the kingdom of God, the eternal state of consciousness. He went to Jesus and asked; 'Lord, what must I do to enter into the kingdom of God?'"

"Jesus answered and told him to keep the law of the prophets as had been written."

"The man told Jesus he had been observing and keeping the law from his childhood."

"So Jesus told him to sell all that he had and distribute to the poor."

"The man was so wealthy with material possessions, and because he did not have the understanding and the knowledge of who he truly was, he was saddened in his heart when he thought of losing all that he had. So he left and didn't do as Jesus had told him."

"Seeing this, Jesus turned to his disciples and said, 'It is easier for a camel to enter through the eye of a needle than it is for a rich man to enter into eternal peace, the kingdom of God.'"

"That's a sad story Ray, though somehow I can understand where this man was coming from. It wouldn't be so easy to sell my business and give everything away." I said, feeling the sadness in my heart.

"This is exactly what I mean Keith, until you are prepared to lose it all, you are far from the kingdom. For when you truly love your neighbour as you love yourself, giving all you have wouldn't be so difficult, because you would desire for your neighbour what you desire for yourself. This is very close to the kingdom of God."

"That makes sense." I acknowledged.

"With practise, you will eventually get this right."

"The Buddha had compassion in his heart when he saw that those he loved and all humanity were suffering. So he sought ways to end all the suffering. He knew though that the solution would not be an earthly one, he had to look deep within for one."

"After spending many days in the wilderness, the Buddha finally got it. All humanity would have to give up **desire** to find eternal peace. This means you would have to deny yourself to live consciously. Exactly as we have said, you should be willing to let go of all that you have at any given point. You should never be attached to anything here on earth.

As Jesus also said, 'If any *man* will come after me, let him deny himself, and take up his cross daily, and follow me.'"

"Again, this does not mean that you do not attend to your responsibilities Keith. This simply means that you know that you are more important than all that is here on earth. Your being does not depend on anything here. And besides, you have access to all that you can ever need, so why seek to hold on?

"A certain rich man in all east once lost everything, even his sons and daughters. But because he understood fully who he was in relation to God, when everyone else turned against him, he stood firm and still echoed these words: 'The Lord giveth, and the Lord taketh away. Blessed be the name of the Lord.'"

It was known long before you acquired this physical body Keith that you would be here. All you've ever needed and all you'll ever need was provided for long before you acquired this body. As we stated earlier from the example of the prodigal son, you need to know who you are. For who you are, determines what you can have, do and be."

"As a matter of fact, you cannot be anything else other than what you already are. You can only forget who you are, and as a result, identify yourself with your thoughts or with the physical body that I'm looking at."

"So living consciously is the solution?" I asked after listening to Ray speak for a little while.

"Living consciously is the only way. To live consciously is to live in spirit. Unless you live in spirit, you cannot please God. That is to say, you cannot please the universe, the all, and you cannot please yourself."

"When Jesus told the multitudes to seek first the kingdom of God and everything else would be added. He did not at all mean that by living consciously things will fall from the skies as with the manna. What Jesus meant was that when you live consciously, your eyes will be opened and you will know then that you already have the 'everything else'."

"Can everyone live consciously though, or is it a chosen few who can live by this truth Ray?"

"Yes, everyone can live consciously, but not everyone will. Suffering is addictive you know. Some people are used to suffering and will not let that go for anything."

"What do you mean when you say suffering is addictive?" I asked, clearly confused by this statement.

"Living out of the truth is suffering Keith. Because you cannot experience eternal peace when you do not live by this truth, you will suffer."

"Suffering happens when you experience any feeling contradictory to your desired feeling. When you expect to generate a specific turnover in your business in a particular financial year and you don't, you worry. That is suffering."

"When you demonstrate love to those around you and they do not do the same, you get disappointed. That is suffering. When your children do not do as you expect of them, you worry. That is suffering. Basically when your expectations in any situation are not met, you stress, worry or get disappointed. That is suffering."

"The only way to end this suffering is to live in spirit, live consciously."

"You mentioned earlier Ray that one must not only be attached to anything here on earth, but to anyone as well, what did you mean by that?"

"Exactly that Keith. You must be prepared to lose those that are in your life to live by this truth."

"How is that possible? Do you mean I should be prepared to leave my family, my children for consciousness?"

"Anything or anyone preventing you from living by this truth is not worthy. Jesus told a man who was preparing to bury his father to let the dead bury the dead, but he should go and preach this truth, the kingdom of God."

"What Jesus was saying is that nothing or no one is more important than the kingdom of God, so if anyone prevents you from this truth, you must be prepared to leave them for this truth."

"Of course this does not mean that you need to leave your family to live consciously Keith, it simply means that you must not be attached to anything or anyone, that you are unable to live in spirit because of your attachments. Nothing, no one is more important."

"When Jesus called his disciples to follow him, he left those who wanted to bid them farewell at home first before they could follow him." "Take a moment and think about this Keith, if you understand what we have been discussing all this time, you should understand that truthfully, we are never without the ones we love. We are one, always."

I paused for a moment to think about what Ray just said.

"You have also been speaking a lot about the kingdom of God Ray, please tell me more." I asked Ray, very curious to learn more about how all this fit in.

"And so I shall." Ray responded.

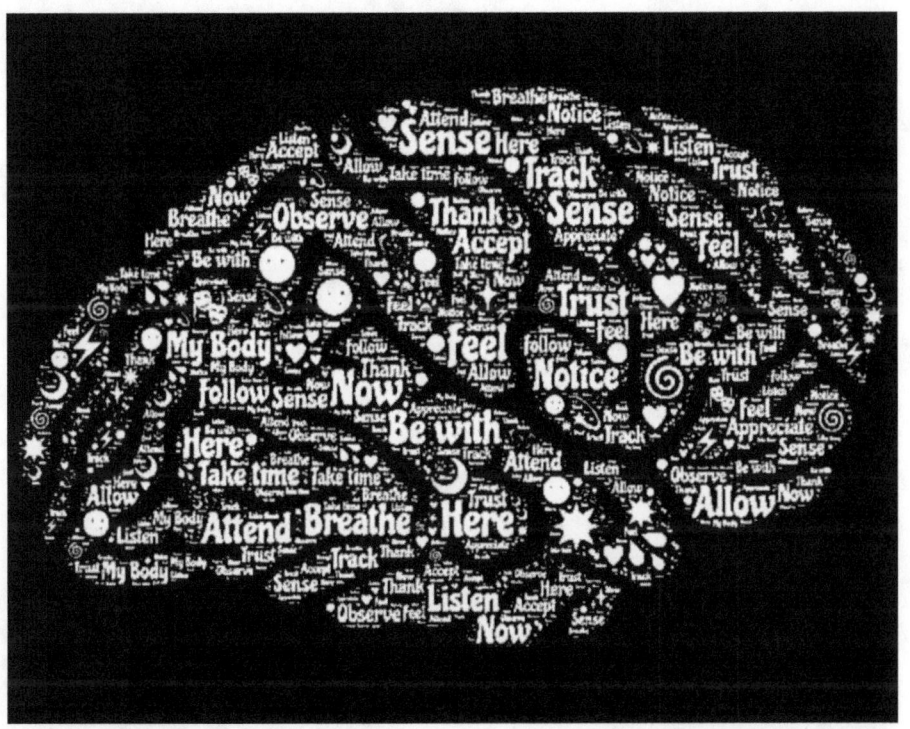

A hobo and the poor rich man

"The kingdom of God is available to you in the here and the now. But the question is whether you are available to the kingdom."

Nhat Hanh

The kingdom of God
"For the kingdom of God is not meat and drink; but righteousness, and peace, and joy in the Holy Ghost."

Ray had suggested that I do not see him for the next couple of weeks.

He proposed that I take some time to apply what I had learned since I met him. Meditation, prayer and daily exercise were a part of me now. I woke up early every morning to meditate and do some yoga. I took walks in the fields and spent some time quietly. I even changed my diet and started eating a lot of herbs and verges.

Those who were around me suggested that I looked more radiant, younger and happier. I must confess that I felt a lot at peace. My days were more joyful and more peaceful than they had ever been. My business has also improved; we have opened two more stores downtown. Meeting Ray was the best thing to have ever happened to me. I am thankful that even though I doubted him in the beginning, I did give him the benefit of a doubt. And now a couple of weeks later, my life has changed completely.

My next meeting with Ray was this morning. I was looking forward to seeing him after so many weeks. He has become a dear friend to me, I have grown to enjoy spending time with him. It did trouble me in the beginning that he was homeless, but Ray refused when I offered him a place to stay. He insisted he was doing just fine.

I have become comfortable with Ray's appearance and the clothes he wore. I was so excited to see him this morning that I ran to give him a warm embrace. I held him for a couple of minutes longer than usual.

Ray was also glad to see me. "Good to see you my friend, you look wonderful. You look a lot younger than you were when I last saw you." He echoed.

"Life must be great in the kingdom of God as expected. There is no other way." Ray continued with a huge smile on his face.

"It is wonderful to see you too Ray, I am at a very happy place. It is all thanks to you."

"Oh no, don't thank me, it is all your doing. I did what I was sent to do."

"Speaking about the kingdom of God, you were going to touch on that the last time we met Ray?" I asked, remembering our last discussion now that Ray has mentioned the kingdom of God.

"I had to allow you to experience the kingdom first Keith, so you can easily understand what I will share with you. And boy am I glad you live there now!"

"The kingdom of God is where you are right now. You have been for a couple of weeks now. It is that place where peace, love and joy abound."

"Are you saying it is not a physical place?" I asked.
"Not at all." Ray replied.

And he continued. "The kingdom of God is spiritual. Love, peace and joy are fruits of the spirit, as Paul told the congregation of Galatia. It is a place where these three are enjoyed in abundance. It is exactly where you are at the moment. You are in the kingdom of God."

"Wait, I thought it was a place we will all go to when we die?"

"When you enter consciousness, there is no more death. Death loses its sting."

"Perhaps we can say, you die in living life according to the flesh and begin to live in spirit. That is when you enter the kingdom of God."

"In the scriptures Jesus speaks about the need for one to be born again of water and spirit to even see the kingdom of God. We are referring to this transformation when the will of the spirit, your will, takes over the will of the flesh, when you enter consciousness."

"Knowing now who we are and that it is not us, but the body, the flesh that dies; if we only entered the kingdom of God when we die, then we would never enter. We are eternal."

"It was written to the Romans: 'For the kingdom of God is not meat and drink; but righteousness, and peace, and joy in the Holy Ghost.' This explains what I've just shared with you. It is not a physical place where you will enjoy all the pleasures of this world, but a spiritual realm where love, peace and joy are enjoyed."

"So all that I've learned all my life about the kingdom is incorrect?"

"This is not something you never knew Keith. The teachers in your life untaught you what you already knew. They untaught you the truth about who you are. The teachings about the kingdom of God were also to unteach you what you already knew about the kingdom of God. I was sent to remind you of all these."

"When Jesus was asked by the Pharisees when the kingdom of God would come? He told them that it didn't come with observation. And he also said
'Neither shall they say lo here or lo there, for the kingdom of God is within you.'"

"If the kingdom was indeed a physical place, the words of Jesus would be blasphemous. The kingdom of God is what you are experiencing right now. You entered there when the will of the spirit, your will, took over the will of the flesh. You entered the kingdom of God when you entered consciousness. Stay there."

"We have already spoken in the past about seeking the kingdom first and everything else shall be added. How has life been since you entered consciousness Keith?"

"Beautiful Ray, beautiful." That's all I could say experiencing so much peace within me.

"Peace, love and joy are found and felt within. Their source is the kingdom of God."

"Have you ever heard someone say, 'Your body is the temple of God'?"

"Yes I have."

"That is to say, God dwells within you, where his kingdom is. He is the source of the love, the peace and the joy you feel."

"I love this place; I love where I am right now. Thank you Ray."

"I have not been seeking to gain anything for the benefit of the flesh since I entered this state Ray. I have only been seeking to remain in consciousness. But a lot has happened in my family and my business. I cannot explain how, but we have been doing great things Ray. We have. If feels like some kind of a miracle."

"It is because when you are in the presence of God, when you enjoy fellowship with him in his kingdom, you must live like a king."

"When you are in this space, like the prodigal son who returned, you are in the presence of your father. You are in your blessings zone. And everything you ever needed is accessible to you. And you can do anything."

"This is exactly what Jesus meant when he said the things that he did and more will you also do. You are in the kingdom; you are with the father. All that is his is yours too. How can you not flourish? You have been made a king and a priest as written in scriptures."

"Remain there."

A hobo and the poor rich man

GOD'S KINGDOM IS

Jesus is King, rewarding, demanding, inheritance, valuable, fruitfulness, God is present, eternal, community, not easily attained, open to all, no place for the sinful, acceptance, heavenly riches, pure, light, spiritual bodies, can be taken away, here and now, not materially focused, inclusive, love of others, unfolding plan, doing God's will, actions not just words, everlasting, promised, can be missed, spiritual, righteousness, unshakeable, Jesus is in control, faithfulness, forevermore, still coming, love of God, privilege, exclusive, committed, powerful, earthly

A hobo and the poor rich man

#

A hobo and the poor rich man

"Oh narrow road of trial and treasure
You're the best road I can take
Though the broad way may be smoother
sparkling glitter and bright lights fake
On the true street light is shining
From the hidden Word inside
But those on the road more traveled
hearts deceived in darkness hide
So when I stumble on my journey
His blood cleanses me from sin
On humble knee I beg His pardon
And He makes me pure within
As I lean on His great mercy
My weakness will find strength in God
Then persuade one on the wide road
To switch the narrow road to trod"

Brian Pettit

Narrow is the way
"Enter ye in at the straight gate."

"It is my desire to remain here Ray. How can I?"

"The choices you make will determine your future Keith. If you make the 'right' choices, they will ensure that you remain there."

"I'm saying 'right' choices here for clarity though there is no 'right and wrong'."

"What do you mean there is no right and wrong?"

"There is no right or wrong Keith. Situations are just what they are. They are neither right nor wrong, it is our judgement of them that determines our views."

"What I mean as 'right' in this context is that which serves your purpose. That which influences your desired outcome."

"So if your desire is to remain in this state of consciousness, in the kingdom of God; what is 'right' will be that which is favourable to your remaining in consciousness. And that which is 'wrong' will be that which produces the undesired outcome."

"I get it." I responded.

"So what is it that is right, that will enable me to remain in the kingdom Ray?"

"Choices Keith, make the 'right' choices, always."

"Jesus told the multitudes: 'Enter ye in at the strait gate: for wide is the gate, and broad is the way, that leadeth to destruction, and many there be which go in thereat: Because strait is the gate, and narrow is the way, which leadeth unto life, and few there be that find it.'"

"Life is exactly like this. Everything we desire, and everything we do not desire is already there. It is how you live this life that determines your experiences. It is the choices you make."

"Two separate travellers were preparing for a journey. None of them knew they would end up at the same destination but both knew all the possible routes to get there. There were two roads in particular; one had all the obstacles any traveller would not want to encounter, but this road was much shorter than the other. The other road, which was the much longer had no obstacles whatsoever."

"So the two travellers made their decisions differently. The first traveller looked at the shorter road and thought that taking that route in particular will get him to his destination quicker. Though he knew there may be obstacles, he thought he had ways of avoiding them. So he took on the shorter route."

"The second traveller on the other hand desired a peaceful journey. It did not matter to him when he'd arrive at his destination, what was more important was a pleasant journey for him. So he took the route with no obstacles."

"So which of these two travellers do you think made the 'right' choice here Keith?" Ray asked looking straight into my eyes.

I thought about this for a minute before I answered.

"The one who took the longer route with no obstacles made the right choice."

"Excellent!" Said Ray. "Excellent."

"You see Keith, it is not the destination that is important, but the journey. Death is inevitable in the flesh. We-the body will all die one day. It matters not when death will come but how one lived before they die."

"The first traveller was in a rush to get to the destination, but he didn't consider that the obstacles on his chosen route would eventually delay his progress and cause him to take much longer to get there. The second traveller chose well. With less or no obstacles on his route, he would likely get there at the anticipated time."

"This is what I mean when I say make the 'right' choices Keith. And you will remain in the kingdom of God, eternally. You have tasted and seen its goodness. It is important therefore that you choose right to remain there. There is no better place."

"How will I know what choices are right Ray, the choices I must make to remain there?"

"The truth is that there's only one choice you have to make Keith. This is the choice that will influence every other choice you make. You have to choose between living consciously and living unconsciously."

"If at any point you choose to live unconsciously, you will have to make many other choices to choose between 'wrong' and 'right'. But if you choose to live consciously, that will influence naturally that all other choices you make be 'right'."

"Just like the two travellers in the example. We can liken the first to choosing to live unconsciously. Whiles travelling on the route full of obstacles, he has to decide at every point which direction to navigate to avoid any encountered obstacles. He must remain alert for the duration of the journey, lest he be affected by the obstacles."

"The second traveller can be likened to choosing to live consciously, as long as he remains on the chosen route, he has no need to worry about how to navigate to avoid obstacles, because the route itself has been designed to avoid obstacles. Do you understand?"

"I think I do Ray, if I may put it my way. It's like a child who lives in the care of his parents, such a child needn't worry about anything for it is all taken care of by the parents. But a child who chooses to leave his household and be on his own will have to constantly be concerned with every step he has to take." "Perfect Keith, that's a great way of looking at it. So your focus should only be to choose consciousness, choose to move, walk and live in spirit. And you will remain in the kingdom of God."

We spent some time sitting quietly with Ray. I was thinking about all that I had just learned and I suppose Ray was doing the same. They say the best way to learn is to teach. So I suppose Ray was also going through a process of learning together with me as he continued to teach me all that he knew.

I realized though that it is all true. As Ray had said, this was not new to me. I've known this all my life. Perhaps I had forgotten as he had said, or sometimes I experienced all this unconsciously, never really paying attention.

There are many instances in my life where I'd decide to change the way I live and live righteously. Interestingly during such periods, I would pay attention to everything I do, every thought I think and every decision I make. It is in those times where life becomes a bliss. I guess it is in those instances where I am consciously one with the universe, where I am in my blessings' zone that all seem to work together perfectly.

These moments do not usually last forever though, and it is only later that I realize that my life is suddenly not producing the desired results, and looking at the choices I make at such times, the conclusion I would use based on what I've learned is, I would have separated myself unconsciously from the ALL. And so this becomes a vicious cycle.

I suppose it is like the story of Jesus and Peter. It is told that once Jesus walked on water and called on Peter to come to him. Peter stepped out of the boat in the middle of the sea focusing on Jesus, and he did not realize that he was literally walking on water because his focus was strictly on Jesus. But the minute he lost focus, he began to sink and he called on Jesus to save him.

So a lesson from this story would be that, when one is focusing strictly on living consciously, on living in spirit; life becomes blissful. This can be likened to walking on water. And as soon as one loses focus, forgetting who they are, living again by the will of the flesh; life suddenly becomes suffering again. This can be likened to Peter's sinking when he suddenly lost his focus on Christ.

So the conclusion from me would be, one needs to maintain consciousness for as long as possible for one to enjoy the blissfulness of life.

"I have started practising what you have taught me Ray, I would like to know the proper way though if you may share with me." I said to Ray, breaking the silence.

"Soon I will share the ways with you Keith, there is still a lot more I'd like to share with you before then. For now, continue doing what you do."

A hobo and the poor rich man

#

"Everything we touch in our daily lives, including our body, is a miracle. By putting the kingdom of god in the right place, it shows us it is possible to live happily right here, right now."
Thich Nhat Hanh

Life in the kingdom

"But as it is written, Eye hath not seen, nor ear heard, neither have entered into the heart of man, the things which God hath prepared for them that love him."

"THIS IS AWESOME!" I screamed out loud walking home that afternoon. I couldn't tell where that came from. It was just how I felt. I felt great! I couldn't care less about what people were thinking around me. I was just in that space. At the same time, I started singing and dancing on the road. Boy I was ecstatic.

I was at peace. I was enjoying so much joy and love within. None of it could be attributed to anything I could see, it was all from within. I loved the space I was in. My life has changed. I am so thankful to Ray. I thought for a second that he had no idea how he'd changed my life, but then I realized that as wise as he is, he definitely knew the effect of what he has been teaching me. It was like I'd discovered a secret to freedom, but like Ray said, I knew all this, I had just forgotten. He came to remind me; to make me aware. He came to enlighten me.

Ray had just finished meditating when I approached for our meeting the next morning. My experience with Ray had taught me so much. Looking at Ray, I wouldn't think he had so much wisdom and enjoyed such peace within, considering that he was a hobo.

Hobos are associated with poverty, suffering and other experiences no one would desire for those they love. I learned not to ever judge people by how they look. I learned not to ever judge at all.

"Welcome my friend." Ray said as he pointed to the mat I sit on every morning during our meetings.

"I have enjoyed spending time with you in these past weeks. You are an amazing chap Keith, and thank you again for allowing me."

"I am so grateful to you Ray. Sometimes I wish I had met you sooner. I appreciate so much what you have done for me." I replied feeling so much love for Ray within.

"As always, I am so excited and looking forward to what you will share with me this morning." I continued.

"The kingdom of God Keith, the Buddhists call this 'The Pure land of the Buddha' it is the same thing. We have touched on this several times already. However, I'd like us to spend some time on this subject. You have already been experiencing life in the kingdom of God, and by your own words have expressed what a blessed place to be it is."

"I love this place Ray." Is all I could say.
"I know you do." Ray replied with a smile.

"There are a lot of things you need to know about the kingdom Keith. The first of which is that it is eternal. Just like you have learned already that you also are eternal, the kingdom of God is eternal too."

"What this means is that you can decide to live there forever and you will. The next thing you must know is that, in the kingdom; love, joy and peace is all there is. You have no needs, everything is catered for. Jesus said 'in my father's house are many mansions and I go there to prepare a place for you.'"

"So when you enter into the kingdom of God, a mansion has already been prepared for you. The kingdom of God has no end and no beginning, so you can only imagine the greatness of your mansion. The streets are said to be of gold there."

Of course I understood that Ray was not speaking about a mansion built with brick and mortar as we know it in the physical sense, but meant this all in a spiritual sense based on what I already know of who we truly are.

"So what's the next thing I must know Ray." I asked showing Ray that indeed I am listening.

"In the kingdom of God is where the manifestation of the power you are is realized. When the teacher said 'I can do all things through Christ who gives me strength', he understood that the power that is in Christ is the power that is in him in the kingdom. Christ is in the kingdom and when you also are in the kingdom you have access to the same power that Christ has."

"Let me explain this a bit more. When one looks at the sea, he points to a little portion of the sea and says this is the sea, meaning it is the whole sea, though he points to a smaller portion of the whole sea. One would point to a different portion of a different size and still say it is the sea. The reason for this is that the water in that little portion is the water which flows in the whole sea, and the water flowing in the whole sea flows also in the smaller portion."

"So if you may liken yourself to the smaller portion, you can also liken yourself to the whole sea. Hence the words of Jesus, 'I am in the father and the father is in me.' The water in the little portion is one with the water in the whole sea, and the water in the whole sea is one with the water in the little portion."

"So when you are in the kingdom of God, you are consciously one with God, as Christ is one with God. When you enter into the little portion of the sea, you get as wet as you would when you enter the whole sea, meaning the power in the whole sea is the same power in the little portion. So the power which is in God is the same power in you. Hence the confidence in the words, 'I can do all things.' Know this truth and you have been set free."

"In the kingdom of God Keith, all things work together for your Good. For you can never enter the kingdom unless you truly love God. For when you are reborn in spirit, you remember that you are love, joy and peace. So in the kingdom, when you set your mind on something, the universe conspires to make it happen. This is the realization of the words written by the scribes to be said by God, 'For I know the thoughts that I think toward you, saith the

LORD, thoughts of peace, and not of evil, to give you an expected end.' This is to say whatever end you desire in whatever journey you take, the end will be as expected, for the Universe, God has conspired to make it happen for you."

"Tell me more Ray, I love what I'm hearing." This was really interesting to me. The more Ray spoke, the more I imagined the possibilities and the more I was prepared to do whatever it took to remain in the kingdom of God.

"In the kingdom of God you don't fight battles Keith, for the battle is not yours but the Lord's. This is what is meant by the words, 'Nay, in all these things we are **more** than conquerors through him that loved us.'"

"I emphasize on the word 'more' here for this reason; to be a conqueror you must compete and win, but to be more than a conqueror means you win without competing. When your enemies think of you, they are conquered before you even appear. This is what is meant by the battle is the Lord's. In the kingdom of God, battles are won for you. Sometimes these battles do not even come to your attention, they are won for you without you even being aware of them. This is the beauty of being consciously aware of who you are. This is the beauty of living in spirit, the beauty of knowing that you are one with God. This is the beauty of dwelling in the kingdom of God. It is written that those who have ears let them hear."

"There exist no impossibilities in the kingdom of God Keith. All things are possible. Jesus once told multitudes that it was easier for a camel to go through an eye of a needle than it is for a rich man to enter into the kingdom of God. They looked at him astonished, they could not in their minds see the possibilities of a camel going through an eye of a needle as big as a camel is. Jesus seeing that said to them; 'with men this is impossible, but with God all things are possible.'"

"Let us spend a bit of time with this one Keith, shall we. If I ask you whether there's anything excluded by the expression '*all things*', what would you say?" Ray paused waiting for my response.

"There are no exclusions Ray, '*all things*' means '*everything*'." I echoed.

"Excellent!"

"So when Jesus said everything is possible with God he meant just that. Hence the reiteration of this by the apostle as we've already discussed; 'I can do **all things** through Christ.'"

"I need you to realize one thing with this. All things include the good and the bad. Therefore, you need to be aware of this. The scribes have written; 'As a man thinketh, so is he in his heart.' Remember what I told you about choices?"

"I remember Ray, choose only that which serves my purpose at all times."

"Exactly Keith. It is important for you to think about what you want to bring to life. Remember, you possess the power God possesses, you bring things into existence. You therefore have the ability to bring all things into existence. So be mindful of your thoughts."

"A man was found dead after he had been echoing repetitively out of fear the words, 'Oh my God I'm dying, I'm dying, I'm dying.' Your thoughts have the power to bring to existence. In the kingdom of God, nothing is impossible Keith. This is what I meant the first time I met you when I said you have so much potential. With this knowledge, you can be what you choose to be.

You can have whatever you choose to have. You can be wherever you choose to be. You are that you are. You will be that you will be for, I AM that I AM."

"In the kingdom of God there is abundant satisfaction. There is no lack. For your father shall supply all your needs according to his riches. Jesus proved this when he fed multitudes with five loaves of bread and two fishes. He proved it again when he caused Peter to catch a great amount of fishes after he had been toiling for the whole night. There is no lack in the kingdom of God."

"I have repeatedly said love, joy and peace abound in the kingdom of God, that is because love, joy and peace is who you are. You only get to be aware of this when you are reborn. And this is just how it is in the kingdom of God. There is no weeping and gnashing of teeth. If you can imagine how the garden of Eden was before the fall of men, all their needs were taken care of. They never even knew they had needs because it was all catered for. That is life in the kingdom of God."

"The fall of men is the point where men forget all this. It is the point where men forget who they are and go back to live by the flesh, living unconsciously. Stay in consciousness Keith, and you will continue to enjoy life in the kingdom of God."

"But why is it so important that I remain conscious that I'm spirit Ray. Can I not know these things if I continue living as I used to?" I asked after a few minutes of silence.

Ray looked at me and responded;

"But as it is written, 'Eye hath not seen, nor ear heard, neither have entered into the heart of man, the things which God hath prepared for them that love him. But God hath revealed them unto us by his Spirit: for the Spirit searcheth all things, yea, the deep things of God. For what man knoweth the things of a man, save the spirit of man which is in him? even so the things of God knoweth no man, but the Spirit of God. Now we have received, not the spirit of the world, but the spirit which is of God; that we might know the things that are freely given to us of God.'"

"This is the reason why Keith. If I put fifty bucks in your pocket without your knowledge, would you know that you have fifty bucks?"

"No."

"You are only empowered by what you have if you know what you have. To know all the beauty found in the kingdom of

God, you must live in spirit, for these things are only revealed to you, the spirit, the consciousness and not to the mortal man."

"If you continue to live by the flesh, you will only concern yourself with the matters of the flesh and never be aware of the greatness you are and what you have because all these are only revealed to you in spirit. Do you understand now?"

"I do Ray, I certainly understand." I had fully grasped what Ray had just explained and it made so much sense. I fully understood. One is not empowered if he doesn't know the power he has. It is written; "My people perish because of lack of knowledge."

"And lastly Keith." Ray interrupted.

"When you remain in the kingdom of God, whatever you do will prosper. As the king David rightfully said in his psalms; 'And he shall be like a tree planted by the rivers of water, that bringeth forth his fruit in his season; his leaf also shall not wither; and whatsoever he doeth shall prosper.'"

"Everything I do will prosper? Every project I engage?" I asked wanting Ray to reaffirm this. It sounded too good to be true.

Imagine how your life would be if you knew that everything you do will prosper, just image.

"Everything Keith, everything you do shall prosper. You will be granted the desires of your heart." Ray reaffirmed.

Ray did mention that life in the kingdom of God was even greater than what he had shared with me this morning. He urged me to remain in the kingdom to experience its beauty in its fullness. He promised also to teach me the methods I can use to help me remain in consciousness, to help me remain in the kingdom of God.

I felt really blessed with Ray, he was like a gift sent to me from the heavens. I was truly blessed by the way he had transformed my life. I couldn't imagine why he would choose me, but he did and I am so grateful. Ray has become a dear friend to me and looking at him, I didn't see a hobo anymore, I saw a very wise master who is at peace with his life.

In fact, the experience with Ray has also caused me to see other hobos differently. I sort of saw Ray in them, I had started respecting them the way I respected Ray. Most of them were probably surprised. I just knew that whom they seemed to be in the naked eye was not who they truly were.

I love life in the kingdom of God.

A hobo and the poor rich man

A hobo and the poor rich man

#

*"Here again I find myself
Always longing, always seeking
Trying to add myself to life's bookshelf*

*Even when I obtain what I think I want
And it seems I should be happy where I am
Some OTHER longing shows its face and taunts*

*I ever find myself straining at the bit
Seeking something I cannot find
Forever feeding the fire ambitiously lit*

*But maybe what I have is beautiful to see
Maybe I should pause a moment and reflect
On all the joyous blessings already given to me"*

Lore and Legend

Contentment

"Not that I speak in respect of want: for I have learned, in whatsoever state I am, therewith to be content."

I must admit that the transformation in my life could not be missed. Everyone I knew wanted to know what the secret was, and the truth is that there was no secret. As Ray had said a number of times, it is the truth we all know and have just forgotten.

I couldn't stop thinking though that applying what Ray had taught me was easier because my life was reasonably ok when I met Ray. But I couldn't imagine how one would expect someone living in poverty to believe that they are peace, love and joy. When one is suffering, how could you possibly expect them to be happy and believe in Ray's wisdom as I call it.

That was the first thing I asked Ray the next morning we met.

"You know Ray, something has been weighing in my head for a while now." I said feeling really concerned.

"How do you expect someone living in poverty to believe in your wisdom? How could you possibly expect one to be happy in such state of life?" I asked.

"I am a happy hobbo aren't I?" Ray said, with a huge green.

"I was waiting for that question Keith, and I'm glad you've asked. It confirms to me that you remember fully now who you are, and that is where your compassion comes from. I can see the concern in your face and that's very good. Thank you." Ray continued.

"Jesus was once asked what the greatest commandment was? And his response was; *'Thou shalt love the Lord thy God with all thy heart, and with all thy soul, and with all thy mind. This is the first and great commandment. And the second is like unto it, Thou shalt love thy neighbour as thyself.'* Your concern comes from the understanding now that you and I are one, you care about the person living in poverty as you care about yourself; that is growth."

"Over the past couple of weeks, I have done what I had to do to bring us to this stage Keith. It is time now for you to meet your next teachers who will teach you the how and give you answers to many other questions you may have including this one. So in the next few weeks, you will meet a number of my dear friends and they will impart even more knowledge to you than I have, to help you continue your stay in the kingdom."

Ray continued as I sat carefully wondering how the next few weeks will be, and the people I'll be meeting Ray refers to as dear friends. There was a level of excitement in me, as I thought that Ray would be the only master I'd be learning from and suddenly it turns out that there are more. It seemed to me that Ray had this all planned out. I still didn't understand why he chose me, but decided not ask, maybe it will all be revealed as time goes by.

"And who will I be meeting Ray?" I asked, breaking the silence." "Soon you will find out my friend. Soon." That is all Ray could say as he stood up and left me sitting all alone without even saying goodbye.

A hobo and the poor rich man

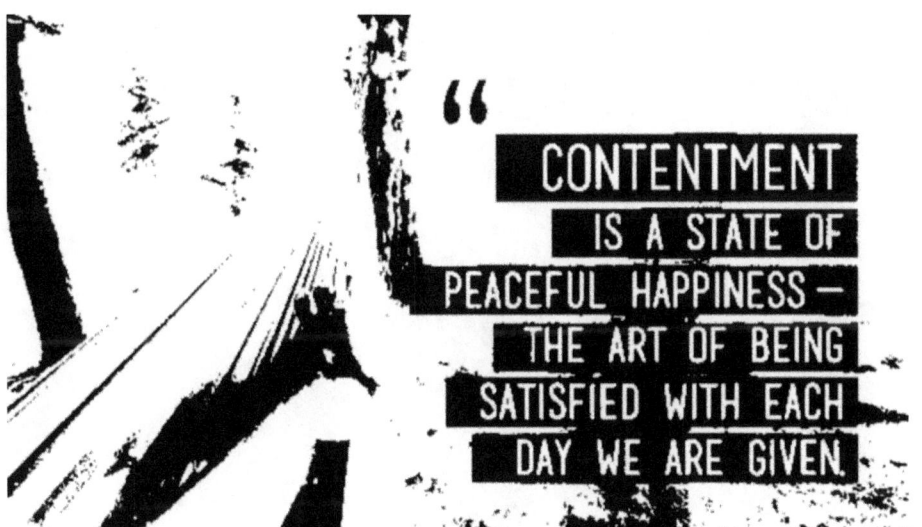

A hobo and the poor rich man

#

Other books:

The Focus – *From walking by sight to living by faith*

Thulani Ngwenya is the world's number 1 catalyst for growth. If you are looking to inspire anyone on any aspect of their lives, be it to inspire them at their job, to inspire them in their faith, to inspire them in their businesses, Thulani is the man for you.

He speaks all around the globe on topics about how to inspire yourself to ignite and keep the fire burning within in order to achieve whatever desired results in whatever task you engage.

For bookings and any inquiry please email:

thulaningw@gmail.com

www.ingramcontent.com/pod-product-compliance
Lightning Source LLC
Chambersburg PA
CBHW062117080426
42734CB00012B/2896